TREMORS

IN THE NIGHTFALL.

ZIYAUL AHMED HAZARI

Copyright © Ziyaul Ahmed Hazari
All Rights Reserved.

This book has been published with all efforts taken to make the material error-free after the consent of the author. However, the author and the publisher do not assume and hereby disclaim any liability to any party for any loss, damage, or disruption caused by errors or omissions, whether such errors or omissions result from negligence, accident, or any other cause.

While every effort has been made to avoid any mistake or omission, this publication is being sold on the condition and understanding that neither the author nor the publishers or printers would be liable in any manner to any person by reason of any mistake or omission in this publication or for any action taken or omitted to be taken or advice rendered or accepted on the basis of this work. For any defect in printing or binding the publishers will be liable only to replace the defective copy by another copy of this work then available.

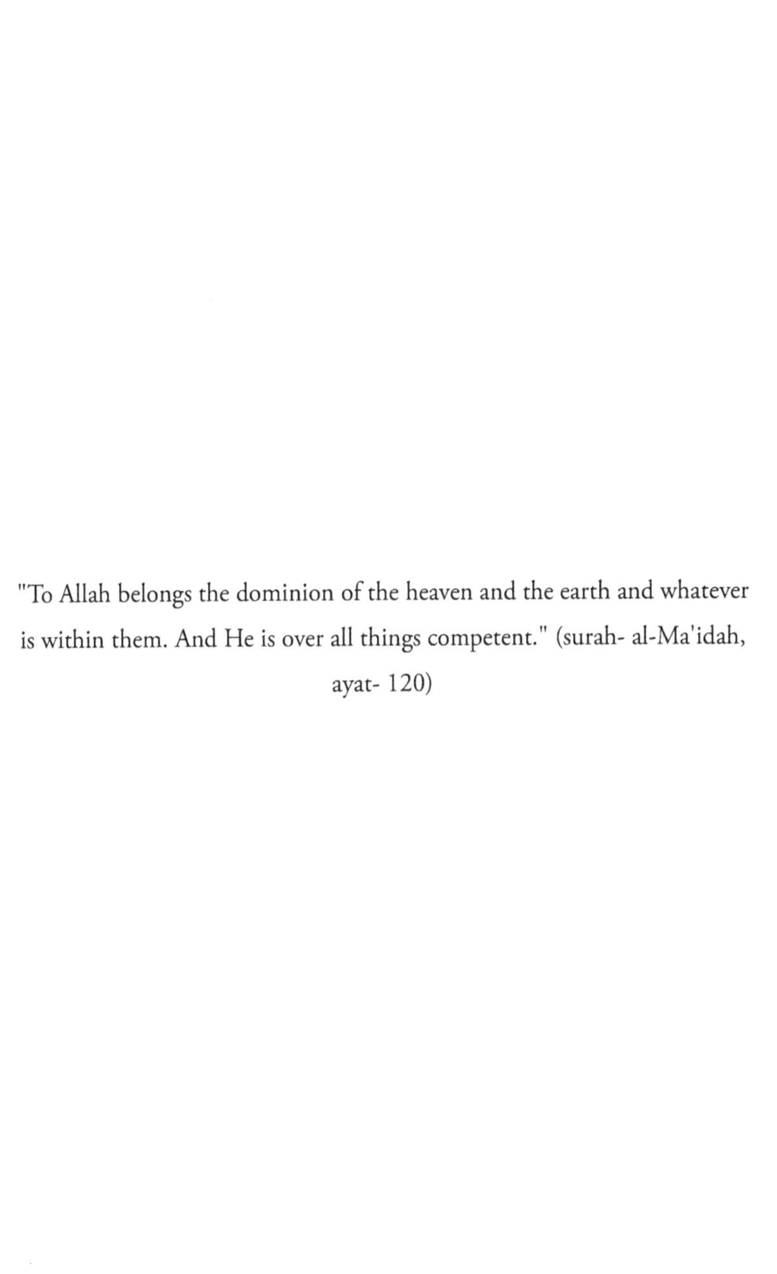

"To Allah belongs the dominion of the heaven and the earth and whatever is within them. And He is over all things competent." (surah- al-Ma'idah, ayat- 120)

Contents

Contents

Contents

Foreword

The whole volume of poetry included in the contents of this book "Tremors" is written by Ziyaul Ahmed Hazari.

Ziyaul Ahmed Hazari was born in Gobindapur Pt-I (Bagehar), a small village in Cachar district of Assam. He is the eldest son of Late Haji Ala Uddin Hazari and Mahmuda Begum Hazari. He was grown up in his grandparent home in Singerband, where he met his everlasting friend Samsad Hussain. His grandfather Late Hazi Azir Uddin lovingly nicknamed his as "Papu". He had his early education in Radiant English School upto second standard and than shifted to Mount Gerizim English School, Kaptanpur from where he metriculated in the year 2015. One day, his school teacher Jiten Singh told his class "Ziyaul can even see what's far there in the Bubon Hills through his wondering mind." It often came true as Ziyaul became a materialistic poet. He is also the Arabic student of late Hafiz Rahamat Ali, late Maulana Rahamtulla and Maulvi Khairun Nessa. Beside he is a bookworm who loves reading. He insisted young minds to read book in all possible time as it provides men with knowledge and wisdom. Ziyaul is fond of playing football, he used to say physical exercise makes men healthy and working makes life profitable.

He joined Gurucharan College, Silchar in 2015 and passed HS Science in 2017. His keen interest to study literature, ethics and history insisted him to persue BA History which he graduated in 2021 from the same college.

Ziyaul is an active student activist. During his graduation, he was elected the Chief Convenor of All Assam Manipuri Muslim Students' Union (AAMMSU), there he worked unitedly with friends and seniors from 2020-21. He is also associated with some other CSO and works for the welfare of his community.

In 2019, his first book 'Abema', a poetic novel in English was published by Notion Press, Chennai.In 2020, with his near friend Samsad Hussain and elderly Salim Mufti, Creative Education Centre Singerband was established. Under their monitorship, the centre impart coaching classes to all primary and secondary schooling students. In 2021, Creative Education Centre was full fleged under the directorship of Ziyaul Ahmed Hazari, Chairmanship of Salim Mufti and Samsad Hussain became the Head of the Academy.

Currently he is serving as an assistant teacher in Royal Public Higher Secondary School, Dolugram. Ziyaul advocated the civilisation brought up by networking mediums. To him, the gaint world can be socially united inside a palm with lots of love through the advancement of technology. Even a students could learn the outside world far away from him and a gentleman can see millions of ways to live, just by sitting in his room. But, he also call upon parents to handle their children with internet gadgets in a proper way. Mishandling cellular gadgets would make children fall into astray.

To him, village life is an inspirational lesson that one could find without a good teacher. He advocated the peace and goodwill preached in the light of Quran and Hadith. He often tell people "terrorist has no faith in religion, Islam is not a terrorism. In fact calling by Islamic terrorist is to blame a peace loving muslim" and condemn terror activities in the name of religion. He also called people to read sacred texts and spread the message of brotherhood. He urge people to lead the short span in peace and harmony. In fact hardship in his life won him wisdom and philosophical approach.

Acknowledgements

In the journey of publishing this book, I pay my humble tribute to my father who inspired me to write. I thanks my mother who is caring and loyal to her children. My family who remains supportive to my needs and fulfillment. My friends, my students and colleagues who always tends to remain by my side.

I regards my love to Mr Mehebubur Rahman Choudhury for helping me with editing and setting up this book. My sincere thanks to Sir Saddique Ahmed Choudhury, principal of Royal Public Higher Secondary School for his extension and supportive hands. I also pay my gratitude to Sir Abdul Hamid Sajabam and Sir Sajabam Taher Ali who are reknowned Manipuri Poets, their writings are ever influencing in my literary works.

I extend my warm wishes and thankfulness to Notion Press for providing me this platform where I could express my immense of innate to this bright and colorful world.

Author

Ziyaul Ahmed Hazari

Prologue

Tremors literally means uncontrollable shaking or vibration. The book is a collection of poetry in English language. It is my second published volume. I had been compiling this book since August 2019 after my first book 'Abema' was published. This collection of poetry are composed by myself and it bears no resemblence to any person or kinds. The poetry includes narration of habitual facts, universal truth, real events, composition, unfulfillment wondering, beauties of love and nature, phases of science and technology and praise to the Almighty. People often speak about poetry as it can be spoken silently and laugh out loud.

The early phase of 21st century faces several challenges of change in socio-economic and political condition which bring choas and disturbances worldwide. Popular protest march opposed to NRC, CAA, Farm Bills, inflation, insecurity, dirty politics, economic crisis, unemployment, hijab bann, hate speech, etc are notable features in India in the 2nd and 3rd decade of 21st Century. Inevitable expression and worst suffering in the two years long battle against Corona made the world weaken. Beside the glimpse of fresh sprout on the taste of monsoon is fantastic to rule again with our pride and achievement. However large scale deforestation and exploitation of green resources made such unending beauty lay hidden from the contemporary society. I urge my brothers and sisters to plants atleast a sapling for every trees we cut down so that our earth remain fresh and green ever and ever.

Whereas achievement like withdrawal of Article 377, restrictions on Triple Talaq, implementation of NEP, Statue of Liberty are highly celebrated all over India. On the other hand reprint of Indian History, glorification of Godse, polarisation of communalism, etc are condemn by a few like minded. National integrity was however moved to thunderbolt, communalism flared up in nook and corner.

All these recurring occurance of talks and fights are widely spread by social media, and enhance people away from their books. Intellectual pay more interest to the institution than having faith in religions. Institutions grew a sense of wealth while moral weaken. It leads to insecurity.

In the Race of Power and occupancy, internal revolt frequently broke out in various countries. In the 20th century, words of civilisation, freedom, education, science and technology were the tools of political institution however there is an U-turn to religious, language, localisation and traditionalisation by accustomed leaders. Thus, the early 21st century is an period of investment in publicity and profits through beliefs rather than testifying the truth.

I share my warm wishes and thankfulness to all readers who are reading this published volume. I thank you for considering your love and cooperation for this book.

Through this book, I requested all the readers and onlookers to stop waging and lift their hands high for peace and goodwill. Together let's make the worldly being safe and happy.

1. ORISON i

Our arms shall raise alongwith
Leafy branches and green goddess.
When the sun swears in its heavenly throne.
When the knights whimpers for their misdeed.
In the varendah of some mosque, some church and some temple.
Yet, the kings of beautiful queens in their merry paradisiacal.
Spake earnestly, laughed hearthily,
While their poor swords run o'er the spear and mayest juvenile triumph.
In a fued for pride and prejudice.
Why doth Thou affaire d'honnour.
Men of Thy world linger.
Waging cold war being baffled .
Alike his ancestral left over,
Whence they folded with their ageing hands,
They stretch the fine scarf upon wooden locker.
A tidy long way to be walked upon
With love and sincerity where malice and amain would scorn.
Men of Thy world would linger.
Making snatch of other hard-earned,
And forget to reconcile kindle trust.
O man of the world at rest,
Come to the prayers orison of conscience.
O cheers selfdom and insight and freed your relentless,

Like a palace with fragrance and melody.
So smile, and abjure the realm.

2. ORISON ii

O tauntless neusis rays,

Shall I call thee a pro domino,

Thee sprung, when the clergy spring rest in her estivate,

And await the approaching of winter,

Yet we opt to rebus ye pride.

Thou dreams shall ever impressed me.

It hush down as the mortal voyage landed.

Oft the sparkle, led and thunder tours amain,

To see the mass wreck of cruise.

But as streaming flash a voice enough to love

Beneath the darkling clouds and waves, then floatsam.

Again I gage the melodious o'er far stretching pastoral.

In gleeful dance sought-

After a harvest moon of thoughtful monsoon rain,

It shall resurrect by a protracted eye dialect.

Though I demurs in pensive vacation.

3. THROUGH THE POETRY i

I write many poems
But this is a kind of poetry.
Through which I speak heartily.
Without lie, fear and smile.
In love with earnest.
Because I know-
You're reading this with a smile, now.
And you would like to ask me "who are you waiting for?"
But again you'd think "why should I?"
For I might caught you...feeling about me!
Than you feel like playing with my hearts on trickle prank.
In this love and care.
I understand a bit of game.
Where you're a heroin of my perfectly choosen.
Our closure is a barrier, and it could break resonably.
That I don't want to be faraway from your sight.
Through this poetry expresses
You and I are taped miles away.
Differences midway, do the love for one another be the sole dependence.
I hope, yet doubted as I don't see conscience.
It is just the matter for my indirect approach
To you, with love forever.

4. THROUGH THE POETRY ii

You're reading again.
With an inflammation,
A sparkling of mind, within your fancy.
"Shall I asked for it!"
Saidst yourself, isn't you.
Happily shook down behind your fairy smile,
Cunningly you want to reflect your preety charms on a mirror face.
And say something more curious than before..... But
Nay, there may be other or course of random.
You thought and left worrying a little.
And now at work, you'd remember me again.
But you don't, well I know not.
With your feeling impatiently praying.
Within which we're rowing on each side yet unknown.
The care that you and I hold infinite.
So now there's a lovely distance being shy.

5. TREMORS i

A world for us, I behold
Tight in their palms they hold.
With uniformity we're napped to silence
A language and common among us
When our words are stripped out of lulling tongue,
Though no bars rode our spinal,
An invisible chain guide our state.
Sometime freely wandering but around a barrack
Surrounded by some Hitlarian paints.
Somewhere we see freedom high up the skies,
When some hawks soar, in its motion wherever directed.
Stressing its momentum over any resistance,
While I'm hiding in the brambles,
Sipping sweet nectar and smashing floral colour.
Almost enjoying the tasteful gift of nature.

6. TREMORS ii

But an imperialistic portrait of weakling.
An innocent myna within coop
Her neck is roped by sharp golden knot,
Her movement is likely to bleeding in its brim,
Her camouflages are painted varieties
And wrap her shedload out of convergence.
Here; a tot lot is decorated-
At the estuary,
from love curve deceivest
from satisfaction to discontentment
and jealousy out of sympathy.
In little things like weight and measures.
The burden being chic, wipe out humanity,
While plot of fertile bank are eroded.
This admiration is an amaze of assumption.

7. TREMORS iii

Abema......! As she flexed upon,
A charming smile beside her sweetness.
She throbed towards and hugs him tight.
At the choirs of twinkling coins.
Then scrunched his solid pocket full of lies,
Just a five Rupee coin, tweeted she in joyful cries,
And turned to her old mommy,
As if her brethren have returned with glamorous wealth.
A drops of tears from mommy eyes.
Boarded to her forehead and at the entrance ran unto her splendid
cleverly.
And lifted in her arms the drape of aging door,
To welcome her son after tedisome days.
Inward is obscure and cold.
There's no window and ceiling down the cache roof.
A clumsy moan, fall from a right corner,
Citing "lord be praise" in a fascinating favour.
A wind heeds upon burning wick, it took the lamp shade where his sick
dad lay, on the same bed and safe.
In his paralysed hand is a bead rolling, once I provide him long ago
Though he couldn't recognise his firstborn desire,
Of his destiny had he dreamt...
She shout in mirthfulness
In her thrust a song of her mood.

I felt and only she could understand.

8. TREMORS iv

A white cloak and a purple shawl crawl off from his luxurious backpack
Fascinated by crick and crackling sound.
She howled from his hand and felt on near lap.
One for daddy and the purple for mommy, softly she flutter.
A pale lamentation turned her face,
Towards dependable ties within a wink.
An appellate package of bluish darling suits for her approaching winter.
She hold and stepped under her cousin's floor
Merrily laughing at her splendid bosom.

9. TREMORS v

Behind the existing fold is a tremor,
A truckling, a wave that pushes.
Thou echoing hills as a boulder, Thy erected mountains as a border, Thou
exile sea as a barrier.
Both day and night are lighted to pleasure.
In readiness all shook to strengthen the power of boons.
At sudden and cruel stretch of wild palm,
Ice melts and lethargy tide rises,
Somewhere with praises and applause excess my joyous mood.
Behind the existing fold is a tremor,
A truckling, a wave that pushes aboard.
A world wider than glamorous pomp and show,
To cause some words of her own,
She's trying to identify herself-
the most beautiful lady borne e'er.
All little face saddened in vanity,
While she wander beneath fortress
Of various aspect of settlers around the blunt edges of harvested farmland.

10. TREMORS vi

Flawlessness marched diurnal
The rising yolk delve deep.
Wherein our silent core submerge.
Sparkling dews upon leafbird, held the roar with her charm of chants.
But the roar being pallid, failed to reach,
And that pulse strike twice and then proceeds,
Until those sunbake beach affords their accommodation.
At least Darwinism could provide essentialities,
Though it failed to deal with religiosity.
When palls of sleep hardly deviate by overrated tremors
Our divine origin isn't more innocent.
Per se jealousy, faraway from mortal sweetness
Behind a grail, like snowflake falling amain.

11. The Nightfall i

The sleeplessness walks iffy

In an oblivion dusk;

de bard anxiously wanderedst.

after a long daydream.

Nights are horrible yet approaching

With shroud terminable tales told by creepy crawlies.

Amid bats and owls truce fled to tarry.

The sleeplessness walks amorously.

O'er opaque floor of faux vale,

We laugh lavishly at her poor endurance,

Then a tractor tilled the tightening gleam

And her keenness observe the juvenile heart.

The brook flow has wiped its virgin berg.

It melts on frolic melancholy,

After all people of the earth accompanied.

The sleeplessness walks along her ambigious.

12. THE NIGHTFALL ii

O there's up the roof
Is a crater mapped by howler.
Wherein,
The twilight dived in,
The faint eventide dripped in,
The raindrops sipped in,
And drive away thou sweet sleep.
A sickle against a dagger drawn together
Stuck on the back of waist belts.
And walked along the water lines.
Tracking miles of merciful lands.
Whence thou gathers bunches of reeds to tire the vacated sole
And a bundle of firewood for our preparation.
Returning on the same route that was heard,
Thee sat upon the boulder and splash about,
And build up unit of pride colour.
Beyond emerald sea, that soar untouch high up the skies.
With an eagerness, the bard moves beneath dais.

13. THE NIGHTFALL iii

There's no force in the smokefall.
To cause a shadow or nature may love so.
Beneath the floated clouds I'm shrank.
Like a rudderless ship.
Nowhere is a movement trembling,
But a swift sound solidifying all sharp edges.
Neither tremor is diligent nor down the epicentre
To wither eclipse of eccentricity.
Lo, humus is as soft as light foothold.
Its utterness minglest with fragrance of wild ingenuity.
When at once the greenery hailse prostrate
A boon of blazing star canst set her merchandise.
Swarm of locust thaw.
On wide due door of frameless wall
Grinds the art of making freshlet,
Within the veil of flory fountain.

14. THE NIGHTFALL iv

Little Doris ascended, holding Oceanus hand;
The newly invented steam worn off hot abscess.
In all frustration from the chimneys.
A fluid that could even mess lava.
Leases raw minerals and flash upon barren plot.
On his humble toes, they stood aghast,
They raise their elastic neck at the galloping.
To contemplate if any form of lure.
When some form of love is yet to ponder.
It squeeze moral sentiment,
To make that something rolled unto our mind, a thing of possibility.
Again and again striking heavenly testament,
In such a pleasing and blissful notion,
Pronounce de sort of archaic,
And accumulate an adequate memoirs of late aegis,
To model an appealing lives.

15. THE NIGHTFALL v

O darkness of moonless hours.

We're on voyage with pole star.

Under eradication, dost gloomy clouds hail down?

From far earth brought an ideal lesson,

For all sectism gazers.

Oft infantry and cavalry baffled o'er travelogue,

While soft flames of wick lamp swings.

In its obsolete century, wicked wing flipped.

A tough eerie but heal leniently.

Baring the dawn music,

The window sill is pulled,

And all scattered rays from shutter fall disdain,

To the bamboo groves growing leniently.

Where sparrows and doves flew out of eastern turret.

Then fall the mercy shower, vide spreading mattress.

16. THE FUN WE HAD i

An academia arise for youth and affairs.
When bigamy ensued within four walls,
Our barrel rings above erratic air.
Throwing swift linen and soft woollen behind bar,
Venom whack across several lurgies forehead.
de mora is highly adjusted.
All praises are triggered anow,
Lough omen laugh at surges,
Forming united and parallel fences,
With faint moral gleams and echoes,
Through swallow pools with pomp.
In faithless wandering during harvest festive.
Within utmost excitement, such an appealing thrust,
Call upon her, an alarming endowment.
Oft shivering thee ravages.
By whose height leap beyond the touch of nightfall stars and midnight
crescent.
From inside a dusty cell,
Some speck of flesh worn out of scattering microbes.

17. THE FUN WE HAD ii

Life is a stream, a steam of bubbles and foams.
With waves lapping her turret
While eroded some lovable sites.
But there's as struggler, providing herself some sort of fortunate,
A voice echoing through and everyone could hear her silence.
In His lively world, both tears and smile
Could hold their breath tight in their palm.
While delivering in it.
In matured potter clay breeds alike dwellers of kind earth,
Enjoin His majestic ideology,
Unlike emptiness made by faith and belief
Though Thou shallth move a mountain.
Ere the worshippers are drawn with logic and reason.

18. THE FUN WE HAD iii

There, I step down the merry dreamland
Like Alice in wonderland.
To feel the warmness for a closet
Against the neveling of sunshine.
Than between two houses,
In a lengthy unfavourable ties
Yet a chain couldn't hold the fragrance tight.
Amidst barren sorrowful mountain
Our sea couldn't engulf the blessed water.
Melting rocks and pavement are covered with snowy mist as untrodden
remains.
Like the two houses and I
Between two family just to mingle, far sight
However a soul to heal two words.
In these pitiable whorl, gathers little thing around insolence,
They'd sought their differences in appearance and acquaintance,
Like nut in stillness but tough to crack.

19. THE FUN WE HAD iv

Up the skies are dark clouds
And underneath flew white beacon birds.
Which maze my mind a kindle towards nature
With loves around beauty, has the nature nurture.
Beneath the breeze out of swelled summer,
Along the rills and across wide cropland.
Where I'm lying down the grassy pad, falls sweet rain.….Ah! sweetie.
O'er grassy arse drops by drops pour down
Until wetness soak up and my cloths stuck me hard.
But as she drips, the ground slips her in
Like a river full of pride.
Like terminator eroding sixes and centuries into long dominion.
Being the domain it lay stretch,
Whereas some bards peep out of turret.

20. IMPETUS i

Not many days,
We hurdle the crossing end.
It had just set into hardly growing woods
Beside the paradise plight.
Hundreds and a river
Are throb for the theist,
And none dare to His dealing wise.
Bound to travel an untrodden lump
Through dusty and foggy wintry light.
Where there's no road and pond to feel dry throat.
But nowhere to settle
Curiously lean up and bade for ever.
Two days in the woods
Eating sweet carob and olive leaves with coconut water.
There's a stream, its water is boiling rotten wild,
Mosquitos and bats nested the saffron bank.
So, made the moving further
On the pricky stone and glazy sand
Under tall trees and thickly sprouted creepers
As the wide way loses.
Sun set in the west reddish sky
When sharp owls rage largely eyed.
There's no lodge nearby
But a palatial leafy shroud

Painted down the mound slopes.
Weary looking around, Ah- just the curly radiant falls pale.
A freak sounded likely "why d hell, you're?"
Being subtle (to whom), turn and look at..!
But found nothing than an impetus of a certain fault.

21. IMPETUS ii

So many days of sour sweat glory be!
After the earth is thrown to foul odour.
An impetus is blown upon a stound of thirst.
Neither as a favour nor against the weird voice.
It knocks the door harsher than ever,
Poaches the locked door of human race.
Being unable to defy mankinde despicable.
Our honorary now abode.
An offensive bolcane rattle on pitiableness,
When omen abiding are sealed behind threat,
When people of the world with their magnificent power,
Render to invisible swift.
As solemn vicelet a manifestation
In terminal approach; blend of humanity and terrible livelihood
....raisest-
"Men make religion, no religion made man."
The imperia of noble corona expands restlessly.
Earnest, conquering rapidly time and distance.
Made colony collapse disorder by his mirth.
And we are engage in war with her fensible,
Laying on of hands thus strengthen.
Unifiedly we shall celebrate jubilant triumph.

22. MEMOIRS i

The memoirs sing in choir
Praise helm and flairs to holy spring
When cuckoo whoop from her little brim.
A pride beside hearth hern.
A glaze but poorling
Her honorific in shanty sage
Aghast thou shivering with cold elf.
Some moron in hurry pay
Dazzle lit from behind the silver lining.
Comical thrum outwit truest blend.
Love returns, like a bag of ferrets.

23. MEMOIRS ii

An old man with his woman,
In a little hut with his little son.
Live happily…from hand to mouth.
Restlessly he works and returns with fifty or hundred
And rejoice their hungry meals.
After the old lady prepared rice and chilly chatney.
They all gather and thank the Lord for health, wealth and blessing.
Everyday it follows, then thankfully scheme was granted-
Electrical post were raised,
Wires were roped from one post to the other.
Water pipes were dugged deep by the roadside,
Motors was installed and water drew from far off river to every varendah.
And all villagers watched the boon of science.
Someday later, every houses were lighted and fan swang down the roofs.
And after hopeful harvest
All men, women and their children lust their precious time sleeping
sweetly.
When after a month the lineman knocks on every closed door.
To wake them up and hand over their billing.
Poor man, they called upon themselves and rushed to the panchayat.
Who read out aloud, "the electric bill for your first month is Rs-…. And
the water bill is Rs-…."
Oh broken down…. as what could I do? how could I pay?
Neither me nor my son are engaged in govt. sector .

Yet He provided us in the form of payment.
How daring, His cruelty is.
We voted for our own cause and their hundreds ofr promises remain
unfulfilled.

24. MEMOIRS iii

A grandeur playing;
Between the old man and his little grandson.
Their chess board seems moving with my long drawn eyes.
It's now half pass twelve yet hunger didn't matter.
A silence between two players sitting side by side
Mirth their importance in hunting one-another dice
Like a predator adopting haunch bone.
Long is the way that shall be conduce
Among the few audience surrounding by
With glaring eyes on descent foam.
Some nodes of kind air blew sideward
And we feel it's eerie.
Amidst warm summer glance
Which swells their pride on freaksome.
Then, I thought….am I loser and should support successful citizen
Seeing someone suitable, I tried to wander insearch of
Being raise and hardly a man I couldn't cope with
To speak an else! nay… a tough job, for a writer
And favourable be; if I shall learn to speak rather than a favour.

25. MEMOIRS iv

A moment for us,

And a choir alongwith,

The coolness of being in summer bay.

May rejoice our movement laying hand in hand.

Through loneliness, an admiration like life and only between lovers.

The solitude of nature yet our passion don't care His optimism.

And wait like the many

Until we see the colourful returns of the doer.

Down the southernmost skies and above sandy floors blew

The wind o'er green and dewdrops silence.

It sow the gentle grains of luck,

Then some kind of tempering wonderbird flew around.

To see some set of mystery in an asset.

26. MEMOIRS v

Mortal men and immortal soul
Land in stillness and transitory waves
On barren remain we do come and go.
O continuity let spatial dispense.
Let ingenuity helm thou.
O malaise of firman, sicken not the poor doer.
Let their works of appraisal cost be our commendation.
Unlike witty birds, they sit not to write ever temptation,
Like willy bird, they soar below average.
Without leverage.
May we with mighty man and desirous sprite,
Glorify our land, wherein lies many of our men buried,
And among them are consolidant of our birth.

27. MEMOIRS vi

A long way, as I dreamt
To walk on the black top, as I desire
Big trees and blooming flowers,
Along the edges grew giving shades,
For poor walkers like me.
No motor-bikes and cars can settle a poet terminal
Rather than his poetry on leaflets or paper pieces.
Neither wealth nor pompous lady grim our heart
Like a beautiful precise of floret nature and prim poetry do.
Despite gain and profit talks about
For three lovely siblings.
Works nor money do we care
For a priceth of happy meal.
Sometimes by a familiar smile,
On her little chick, could make my day.
Amidst variant colour and passionate odour
Tis' erring on the side of amicable.

28. MEMOIRS vii

A marvelous nature full of awe.
Suffice with beauty and malice
For akin and beloved, appears dissatisfaction beneath barest.
For love and jealosy, appears discontentment beneath malevolent.
For wanderest and lone Survivor, just a moment of loneliness and
nowhere to abstain.
And a moon in stillness, shading sorts of even tide.
And a road which is mine and I walk on.
But the darkness belong to them, who settle with lights beneath beautiful
houses.
Yet the sky filled in air is independent,
Not mine, not yours, are we sharing our breathe.
When downpours, swell our great river
He sumerge mighty lands and all strong hands stab in their melodic.
Lo, we bewail; though hapiness and joy ridden hereabout,
From earth we grew and shall we return
To recompense, then on earth where we once lived.

29. MEMOIRS viii

A man as gentle as poet
And worded like a poetic beauty.
River and dales with their sweetest nectar
Oft humming treeline with beehive
And flowerence blooming the acre of maturity.
Behind the wall of mortification
Prayed in fear; whorl eyes and crawled hand,
Thou_ my Lord the beneficiant!
My way from earth to the town of naked soul
My walk with fashionable outdraw to be a bare fanthom.
When I had to drop off the trigger between the aged life and sprouting
dead,
I remember the kindness of rain in the midst of summer,
I remember the stretches of warmth blanket and eve fire in the grasp of
winter.
And wondering if I'm the holly abode of seasonality
That's feeling the tune of early chants of the bright sun, twinkling star and
faint moon.
Which weren't felt by anything around.

30. SILENCE i

Silence haunches
May witheld our lamentation.
But working men may return with pride of being observed
In a glad afternoon.
With warm tea and sweetened mouth.
That speak pity but breakin wonderful party,
If the world is so beautiful to harness.
Like the charms of dark eyed
Laid on colourful garden around luxurious hut.
It is a world of word.
But many words may break the torch of unification.
Winner are those who spake,
And tears may flown on the loser indemnity,
While serving the bourgeoisie in winter eve,
Happiness are the warriors in pride.
Down the gleam of stroud and highflying rainbow.
Could men behold frozen foams, marked by adjustable Lords.
Nay, a bard could've misfortunes by an errand.

31. SILENCE ii

In the midst of tough wind,
We're shivering, the frozen peak of silent night.
Lone but shall a wonderer,
Ever imagine the trauma of woolen kits.
In the faraway woods and down the deep shade.
Splendid are the untouch glance.
O ever watching eyes, hast thou seen the admire of pride umpiring.
Lo, men of thy earth will laments,
Whence a vergin soul swells.
But it dampen and will only forge.
May mayor of cities and Lord be abound,
Together in the joice of popular voicelet.
So it maintains the adour of initiative again.
And when I lie on the surfaces of plain faces.
Oft innocent wind blew to affrim the thesis of flounce,
Those faces whom I see long days ago, charming and lovable.
And now reviving, mimic trust, within the glaring.
Though men live or man die, sympathies rinse the eventful series.
It shall risen heavy irises
Into a wide viewing temptation.

32. HOW HAPPY I AM i

How happy am I when I was a little boy
Going to school with a bag and a rupee or two in my pocket
How happily do I step in?
Wishfully thinking of sweet chocolate.
Happily we walked in the rain, on the muddy floor
And under the sun, on the dusty sand
Every Sunday morning, the joy of holidaying with friends
Happiest are we in our village keen observed.
There is no tension of earning under the comforts of rich daddy.
No burden under the care of kind mommy
How happy am I?
In the scenario of pity memory.
And now flashes of flakes upon me
To work in order of earning our satisfaction and goals
Linked by the perpetual knot between limited time and space
Maintaining the bond of love and duality to affectionate dwelling.

33. HOW HAPPY I AM ii

The night passes as I am and swiftly like herald tales
With favour from Mommy and Daddy
But not a penny rather to work, earn and eat.
They let me educated and bless me with the wealth they have
Indeed I grew up wanting to be an Indian
Many a night passed away in sleeplessness, with the disciplinary voice
insought
Wandering if I worked hard, Insallah I will March leading brave
contingents.
But have I seen barriers and some wealthy men held the bridge of
highness,
High up the arena and they crossed upon
And I lay on the floor under the faint lamp light
A book side by me, a pen on my hand and on a notebook I wrote
"If my parents have send me to a potential centre"
However I didn't realise what's my homework.
But now I know that
My parents on sickbed, and happily are my little brother and sisters
In great hope of my return,
Yet my walk to safe landing still walks an effy
But the charming of daylight still hung me high up
Unlike ages of great Roman, had I am the only undies
Either happiness or the joy of being in family had I to decide
Beneath jewel heart, decorum sought fulfillness

And I do returns in pulses, other than else
Of a poor and happy family will I shatter.
To thousand ashes of love and love around.

34. HOW HAPPY I AM iii

(To uphold the integral liberty
A poor man could do an enough hours.)
I'm a divine creature.
Borne on earth and here settled.
With life run by blood across my flesh and bone.
Which're again twirl to sand and pebbles,
By decomposer than liquified to coal and gases.
So could I feed until my jealousy felt satisfied.
And men nearby shall speak about my might
And strength of mine besought from the far east to gravel west.
Whereas winter's coldness, burnt meat and woolen shawl
Even lighten the flame of Bharti workers
That shine so bright as crude oils wick,
Spills on crop field and burns happily at a blaze.
O poorness, harness not,
Only horses run to pull heavy chariots
Unlike the steam engines, those are fueled with wealth.
Barn and tame called upon tired evening
Healthy labourers laid o'er greenish meadow,
And themselves refreshest with a warmth beverages
Than felt to sorry, oft exhausted with wandering dream.
Not a good childhood should I be fearing;
Or a good route should I choose to life and luxury.
But how! Just in a hardly maintained road

TREMORS

I'm reckless to the doubt of seasonings.
Erring to choose one amongst, yet I find it nevertheless
Whilst will and powerest that acclaim temporary being
Nowhere surrounded with raised border or bared sea or barren desert.
Yet, the difficulties of fulfilling a pride
Remain timid between negligence and habitual facts.

35. HOW HAPPY I AM iv

I am a poor man.
Who wanderst alone and along ye ligneous of poetry.
But poorer than me was the orphan I met,
Near my house, he'd stayed there and years before I settled.
With lively courage, without woman and descendent.
Awe! in his earning are,
Big friends and children wail nearby.
Affectionately on the tide of luxe sundial.
Gathering wealth and power, to pacify
An era of swiftness, fluently passing on all occupancy.
Yet its reflection are however improper
But a fatigue wave could blow them to lust,
Unless erected to high raised fortification .
Well, being without a platform
He shun all hopest and desirest.
There I could see the opposite bank of Barak.
His solitary house standing on stillness,
With resourceful business of day and night,
Led by some doers between two akin hearts,
They tills and tilled the land until a treasure reach,
The feasiblity being ignored, however his return impolicies.
Many a factors, though in pensive fair.
Later or even by priorities, rather than a silence conveys.

36. POTYOM

Her last wish
THERE; in the bazar of Singerband
A little child,
Grey and curly hair, pale skin, and fairly smart as three
With a torn bag she'd came and slightly heavy in her warm expression
ana-return with it, however as sun set in, her little charm losses.
What might be there? Is she selling well?
Might be delicious palms of winter and juicy mangoes in summer
These are easy fruits in our deciduous wild garden. Whatever be!
Let my intention do not interfare her businesse.
And many a days I kept watching from the window of my academy,
The routine of her materialistic world.
I thought she's selling prettily and a lovable girl is she
And could enjoy a margin of happiness.
Impredicative day being with some Rupaiya
I went there pridely but with a heart full of words.
There I could see the little ones sitting in a corner
On a torn plastic pad she raised herself against the wall
Under a roof that could be blown in any light wind.
I hope I could buy something by money but....
She decorated, the clumsy. Oh goodness
Broken toy cars and poor dolls, some biscuits and snacks, a few worn out
clothes and two bundles of firewood.
Which the rich men and women gifted as a motion of kindness.

Wonderly arranged in row and column,
As if she is selling in. But who're buying?
Money for her goods that worth or just a sympathetic payment in loves.
I measures the tongue of hardly earning and heard the call of viz.
But no kindness is fairer than making her elite workshop a hopeful
harvest
Then, I paid her a hundred for a toy car and a doll.
But she refused in wants of two counts for two things
More or less she didn't called and after a quarrelsome bargain
I see some scattered people around us who talks illicit when I pass on two
notes of fifties
To make her day, a happy earning for hard work.
(Note: Potyom is a manipuri word meaning baggage. This poem is titled
as Potyom in Manipuri since the whole pictures of this poem reflects about
a poor and orphan Manipuri Muslim girl trying to earn a little by selling
her broken toy and leftover snacks in the bazzar of Singerband-
Cooperative, a village in the Lakhipur Sub-division, Cachar, Assam.)

37. KHAIR

(Kidaba yade meoibgi mathouna,
Pangal kallignai, thamoigi aningba
Pangthokloidba krisu leirmdre.)
. . . . . . .khair. . . . . . .khair
Even high up the sky
Lurks his name,
By an eagle soaring.
His premature death; is offen
Though he could breathe till his last wink.
The surrounding doesn't want him alive,
So tuck him off from their happy being.
Men zeal over wealth is an existing realm.
In this world his richness may wreath,
Just to obliviate mannish poor birth.
But! Why shou'd one hanker after possession?
Hereafter he'll pass away and loss to eternal sleep,
Tied by pieces of linen around lamentable soul.
Neither luxuriance nor for alms, he'd imagine in a dias.
Note: Lines enclosed in brackets is a lyrics composed in Manipuri on the
brutal killing of Khair Uddin. It is translated as-
"Man courage is fearful
There's nothing impossible
If ye desire and strength suffice."

38. A SONG OF BLINDNESS

A wanderer....there

And I wonder who's she?

Neither I see her ere, nor does she called upon.

A man trying to approach by his neath.

For travelling some length down to the miles of ages,

With the choir of long memoirs, childhood and youth affairs.

Then, only a word she speak off.... Like 'where'

And keeps walking but with a smile.

On her face that I hardly caught from her childish.

May be the lady of my choice and she might be a pride where I could lie

Rest of my life, swiftly and blissfully.

The man of long desire, he could settle desirably.... That we may hope

But no....... To impress her enlight,

Before expression of heart and feels,

It burdened though a joyful ride.

Oh amnesty, seen by lordly and willing

Some words filled with flowing blood,

But who care the rosy at woods whereof sworn the palatial jewelled crown

Pardon! Only a blindness could choose the scent of sweetness.

39. WHEN I DIE

The wind and rain

In jealous felt of being alive.

The rains watered the little ones

Enriched them with strength and wild music

But the strong wind fall down tall trees

And splash the softly growing sweet nectar into rivers of torn tears.

After splendid hours feeling soft breeze under golden day light and

hardship torment.

I think, I will also return to.

For I'm a belonging of Him, this mighty land and spritual faith,

So when I die,

Buried me in a loyal grave (as taught by Muhammad SAW).

Let there be no competition,

Of doing and undone and whatever earthly established.

Dear brothers and sisters,

My beloved sons and daughters,

Cry not, let not your tears falls off on the ground

Cry not, for your tears will make the ground wets and heavier upon me

And I'm afraid if it shall break into my rotting body.

Even before the darkling strom shatters the silver lining into a downpour

And bathed my buried expense that my soul could look and smile upon

purification.

My dear brothers and sisters,

My beloved sons and daughters,

Beleif me while fearing our Lord.
Makes Him happy until the dawn and don't tell to people before the dusk.
While doing things and perform your holy work within an smile.
Speaks out with love and commemorate my glance as a helping hand
Seriously publish not, while serving needy friends and noble children.
Happily fulfilling theirs dreams will be a happiness of mine
Those are my favourite companion, and I befriend with.
Toast them with their daily bread and make me not in hunger strike.
For my hereafter life, now I have many affluences
Of rich and beautiful lively walks, dealing kindly and honestly
I want your subservience, to feed me with honour and pride
My everlasting desire..... May you all be happy and luxury.
My sincere declaration..... I had forgiven all ill and malevolent that I felt
for other.
And lastly I prayed..... Forgive me for whatever wrong I be a doer.
And I sought for peace and unity amongst dwellers
Behind every existing secrecy I left this letter, so the hood shall exist in
everlast.

40. EXALATION

That's a brim designation
Though not a destination.
Our people and all around weep
To the splendour of Almighty
Some stood in exalt
But who move loyally with tunes of sovereignity?
Wealthy and loving
But, I prefer not,
I wanna joy bore of heartiest claims though poorest.
I thought we could withstand the modern impetus
Honestly and kindly, with an ability to sacrifica for a betterment.
And thought we could be affectionate whilst dealing
Before His highness.... we may be lucent.
Thus I prefer over all men of Thy world
To be happy and contented on whatever possess.
A man with his only lady to shed whatever possiblity
Upon their children with love and care,
And in return, hold a ward of kinship.
A well and pleasure dying, then away to heaven.
The place of fulfillment for all hopest and desire,
Wherein no accountable for deeds upon the doers
Like on earth, sometime terrify with horrible calamities
Beside happiness earn with hunger
Till the luxurious strike on pity victory or on some sympathetic gifts.

41. AT THE VICINITY

At the vicinity.

Withheld the torment,

Raised as natural raid,

In a test while on earth,

For afterlife, to prove our rolling faith.

Sweetness being lonely and lovely to hear

Thou expresses in the midst of a Spring night.

While I'm fallen tough to work at daylight

And weary sleeps by early night out of tiredness.

Agony Summer and Winter marked hopefully

To see the setting of Cuckoos on flowery treetop

But I failed, for more a vocal of cries in desperate

Strike on my eardrum, making me a deaf to love and beauty.

In this swear my youth, I search my consistency.

Swift flow of water at steep

Deep watch of catcher from the standing rock.

Tossing of florets crown and chirping of song birds.

The bathe in sprinklers, down the waterfalls.

And joining into a rills behind the velvet hills.

Mesmerizing views are they.

The appearance lasted long as the viewer appreciated it.

Mightily made charming things and are laid everywhere.

But beneath faintheart, would thou feel our unspoken words

Our words of jealousy and betrayal while making up for ourselves.

And our pains gluten two gulfs by expressing latent joy and duality.
Hiding enough fear while making it viable.

42. HISTORIAN

We seek and write

To unify, exposing the realism

And worshipping the true net of goodwill.

Behind a handsome of men, we try to unveil.

The pall, covered centuries ago.

Soiled under the earth steam.

Heated and turn down to lead and fossils.

Yet, lighted brightly when gross and burn on a torch.

Neither an evil nor a devil

Kindle a lamp and bow before.

A lordly affection and mighty charms

Upon we sprinkle incense sticks round a lifeless bare dream.

Invention and discovery is a matter of workaholic

Though by oppertune ignited them a sudden pride.

For some rarely thinking minds,

Living in with ransomware

Orderly recording Einstein's excentricity.

But historically depicted and praises Thee

Why don't we put our education to build up the wonderful past.

While on earth and live as terminal.

Historian wrote about victory and exploitation

And holinesse laments reading the notes of World Wars.

Historian wrote about love and unfulfillment wandering

And made marriages, a unification of true minds.

Historian wrote about pain and glory
And focused the talented to their best performing arts.
Historian explore to make the worldly flow in small nips,
Though a few like Einstein writ 'History isn't a subject'.

43. MOREISH

In my small garden I planted,
Some little climbers, herbs and shrubs.
Within hopes I shall built my charm and welcomes sweetening chirps.
Lo, mystic men.
Now,
the cock doddle and the hen lays
her snacky-slicy white rolling eggs,
inside my cottage, lies her coop,
before the cattle rumble on
our meadow for their greening,
and the plants bore juicy drops of nectar
from ripe fruits and silky flowers.

44. O HEAR ME

Either stranger or familiar.
Tell me who's foreigner on His holy Land
O hear me;
if you're falling by your faults
O listen;
Who're visitors in His holy kingdom?
The mighty emperor or his weak subjects.
The loyal courtiers or his brave knights.
Neither you nor me
In this laid, we're bound tight,
You issued order and upon us entangled
And we worship, ensue to make ourself dependent
On you and to Thou laws for benefaction.
Oft human as an integral
Seduces to wealth and luxury, then fame and occurance, fate and pride
Eagerly annexing the greed of hope and desire.
Facto life but across the lining could we surf.
Nay, all occupancy are swelled by pleasure of wine and women.
"Now, remember my words and promises, "said Ceasar.
Hegemony and their sentenses are only fulfilled
By their deeds and its authorised acceptance.
Because among the many men,
There are some men who can make the nature behave as they wish.

45. A FERRET

Florescent screen

Had my mighty emperor seen us in His holy Land.

The beautiful image of Thine on a magical mirror

That shook His charity upon our worldly and hatch.

Little men to look at it.

While I and you are knocked by

Some harshly powering and eventuality

The truth being percieved, some of us are left unexpose

As we're left with tucked off tongue.

May I die with the last breath;

In the land of my birth and pride.

Will I be buried between the graves of my ancestor?

And among my brethern.

My place being a lovable.

Risen on green vales and above blue water,

Song birds flying out of its turret,

From spiny brambles, leafy florets,

That cherish the world with magnificent.

Then set down yellow meadow and under green water in solo,

All birds and farm animals returning to

Expecting a better tomorrow.

I could see around me

Farmer and fishermen are happy like my poetry.

The moody face of school children

Troblesome walks of busy businessmen
And tiredness of government officials.
But today,
Amidst the concern of rapid rising.
The covid lockdown of city and states.
No one seems to be here,
With no money and no words,
All are troubled in the hardship of inflation.
And amidst the tragic,
Who shall speak on?
Neither I nor you,
Who can stand up like a ferret?
A ferret who had none to care upon.
But me and you, we have our family
In a family where every mother and father like to see their childly sons
and daughters.

46. MY FRIEND

My friend;

Though u stood on the another bank of Barak.

We could see the knot between light and darkness,

The shines of sun, sight of pale moon and shooting stars,

And remember those bond of fraternity,

We troll along swift rift, glamorous meadows and beside the low hills.

Sometimes a smile, somehow smaller than our curious cries

For unfulfillment wandering.

But my daddy stayed indoor,

For one and half years on the same bed.

Still enjoying by looking and hearing us,

Poor faces are we that he knows well,

However rejoice his heart by our rich plays.

It makes me lost in a wonderway.

A mindless land with no suitable thought to bear,

And so lone to be a dreamer

A forerunner for money and faithful pays.

But an ownerless man I may be,

Owning the hardship of a wrecked ship,

Midway between poor birth and sensible death.

Lo, in wants of honour and pride I may be honest

Enough to set my zeal on your dom.

47. THAWAI

Which of the favour of my Lord will I deny,
The freeing from burden to realise my dreams.
Or the favours leading to an attainment of my salvation.
Or the way which my daddy stood by my side.
Or the favours that a lengthy road stretch to my destiny.
So, which of the favour of my Lord will I deny.
Lo, I'm choosen to be unexpected trump.
The way, my daddy returns,
From earthly settling in love
Comfortably dwelled with joy.
Amidst wonderful walks of life
To earn transparency of being holiness and acclaims,
By his honesty and wisdom.
And than returns to his parmanency,
By eternal sleep will he meet his little daughter and loving parents.
The way he returns and left us,
Leave us in sorrow and premiere distress
Through a familiar family we are barely vacated
Into a foam of loneliness that sprung at once
With some drops of purest tear falling amain
From every onlookers eyes at thou finale motion.
The way he return and set to motionless,
At the cessation of his splendid duration,
Celebrated by our traditional and religious rites.

We're deft, dump and blind to his majestic dealings,
Is he hearing, speaking and seeing us and around?
I yearn for his heavenly and peaceful resting in peace.
And I wonder, he be proud,
If we pray for his soul,
If we lives in his accustom,
The way he long for us to travel.

48. LAMENTATION

Some poetic lines that want so,
Amidst plight of patients be,d
Away from the walk of fresh air.
Immence joy brought into the vacancies of noblity,
Here I foresung, the lamentation.
Of beauty, amidst natural bounty that pretend
To be perpetual with my solidarity
When floated on the vastness
Of bottomless sea in a lifeboat but without a row.
No hope could swept the bitterness of life
And there I found my way to strive
Till the reach of half an illusionary.
The dreams of those marketers
From where I buy some fouls by pride
Lone but aware of the love within which I fell
To uplift the jewels of crowned forces.
A straight road and here I stood.
There are two sides I could looked at,
There are two ways I could passed by,
And two different words I could speak on,
For two purposes that could fulfilled my needs,
But unlike the eternal air I'm a material.
And though the water flows downward, life is profitably adjustable
So I stood there, as certainty oppertunate man fortune.

However;
Poems are decorated by the flapping of bird's wings,
By the sea of sweat forged by naturalistic charms.
Though the poet adjusted himself in barren or conjested land.
But;
The philosophy that makes man move
Is marked by his holistic.
Towards;
The solace of diversion
Relics form in dogmatic ideal
Are without my consent and I'm not force to flee free
Sorrow;
Are those in-dependent soul
That remains and floated elsewhere
Even after the body buried to an eternal sleep.
Meanwhilst;
Within a whorl I found myself
Fitted loosely and jerk around the revolution
And let my kin passest by.

49. RAIN

Rain, Rain,
Rains on the green leaves and grasses,
Rains on the woody trunk,
O rain,
rains down,
To fill the irrigation tanks and farming holes,
O rain,
rains to the thirst of farmers,
And we shall be blessed with tranquil harvest.
Rain, rain,
Rains down the streets and passage,
O rain,
rains down and make a swiftly flowing,
Paper boat and match boxes on the minute stream,
Dry leaf on little water,
Sails by a multitude of naked children.
Rain, rain,
O rain,
rains on the roof top,
Above the window still,
Let some droplets fall on decorating bushes
O rain,
rains in the summer eve,
Downpour and shower shall provides a bit of relaxing.

O rain,
rains on the blue mountain,
Rain, rain,
rains down the hill slopes,
Submege the dirts of foothill and reverine plain,
But not in anger and frustration,
Cause not a terror on dwellers by a rapid devastating flood.
But Mercy upon us with fertility for crops and growth.

50. RUNAWAY

In bitter waves,
I am sailing in.
With my row weeping in thrust,
I knew that poise yet none of you care.
My lives and my walk will you say,
That too I knew, but you even don't remind me.
After risking in such situation
I'm afraid of premature dying,
But else would make me dishonour,
Unbearable and hard lives,
And that one, I don't like to be.
But if
I'm successful,
I'll be befree
With wealth and honour.
In such situation
Shall I hid and crawl,
Such that radial ill bid me.
Or shall I raised up to walk,
So that I be recognized for potentiality.
The old man on the night street,
Aged in hunger and mad with many dreams.
Shall I ask him all about.
But how shall he advice me,

He's a runaway man,
Away from family and friends,
Being defeated by the sorrow of life.
But tonight, shall I listen to his words?
I feel and could see this natural march.
Then His calling me, standing by our entrance.
Now shall I response to his call,
O yeah.... Let his wish be fulfilled.
And I hope I could do to serve him a day.
Oh surprisingly, I wonder
How he's so faithful to my deserving.
I could find in him and all my answer are those he saidst,
Perfect and applicable in high respect.
But why didn't he be loyal to life and settlement?
For some men, life isn't like the thought of all woman.
Freedom and liberty isn't that rules and follows.
It isn't a bird that will fly high, and may shot down at anytime.
You are alive and free
To live, to go, to sacrifice, to remain secret and etc
But if you are ruled upon or if you are ruling on other
How can freedom is about happiness and well being?

51. BUT

Sitting on the raise shield of a pond,
When the sun rises towards the day.
I kept watching the charming of ladies
While she's fetching water to subservient.
But,
I may be writing this poetry with a pen.
Which is more sharper than an edge.
"How beautiful you're" thoughtful silence spake.
With the 2 years old baby in her arm,
Whose looks is just his father appearance,
Innocent and seems never be betrayed.
Thus, I prayed for his life and happy being.
Proudness though not be.
Not the facial beauty, let some eyes admire,
Upon the expression, let some hand stretch,
To thee honour and unseen accumulation
The victory of noble heart and the glory glared by kindness.
Being worldly, joys and sorrow be,
Man and socially praises to.
Her darkness within which you pay,
Beauty and bound in her elite charms,
Magnify leafy branches of brambles gateway.
From manhood to a saintly nonelite.
Gentle soul, a heart with timely beat at ardant.

ZIYAUL AHMED HAZARI

A man in the wood
Provided by his rich green and fleshy sorrounding.

• 67 •

52. GRIEVANCE

The joy of togetherness at this baring pain of separation

Am I the only one suffering?

Among those seperated brothers and sisters

So, I lean up with unprecedented smile

So, my brother moves away and wisely to his journet

And he did not weeps after departure.

But lonely will he be there

Just as I shed little tears in a darkling corner

In a new place with new people.

He shall be a stranger and hard to adapt.

His immaturity may sing at a deep touch

Missing his family, friends and the extreme being of Farhin's playfulness.

And here I am "the one man of a family".

Beside a happy motion, fascinated by their cunning smile

That always hinted towards honesty and simplicity

Like the little children who came to me and learn new things.

The toughest lured me to their joyful rides

That I feel happy in its ever smiling sight.

Like my sister slept in loveliness in my early morning,

I hope I should work and support their pleasurable hours last long.

Their welcoming face in my late return

Late than an evening with a small package of the day.

Happiness are blushes of pink roses and sweet nectar

Down the blue skies on velvet greens.

53. Lan Dhan

Lan lei, mee lei.

Daulat lei, taaluk lei.

Peise lei, lai lei.

Leijadba singi awatpa lei.

Hae Prabhu, why this thistlelike

Only in barren barrel.

The striking of clock hands along with brits of my heart

While so lonely, and merrily dance in misc.

The dance of nature's pride

In soft music sweetly sang by birds and woven nest.

The sun, moon and stars are elite objects.

They look at me and genuinely provide me

Their lights and beauty unto happiness.

A bit faraway from darkness and

Everlasting joy brought by its beauty and reflected towards the dale.

In monsoon skies, clear and free from black clouds

Shines the portrait bright.

The sovereignty of cold temperament,

Wintery nights and snowy brow of all brown trees

Harvest the solidarity of faithful accompaniment.

Midnight owls and black bats soar across the sky.

So shall we celebrate down on earth

Riding on a bullock cart

From hills to valleys, crossing running stream.

(lan is a manipuri words which means wealth, whereas dhan-daulat means enormous property. In the 1ˢᵗ five lines of this poem 'Lan Dhan' the poet potrays the will power of wealth Manipuri. He says if there is wealth, there are people and your rights are always receiving but the poor have many unfulfilling, and asked God if He is seeing and hearing all oddities.)

54. FAIR POEM

The fairness of a poem
Surge like a lady of my fairness.
Always to her erring beauty,
And likeness of my reading,
Happily to its content,
meaningful verses like waters flowing,
Lively depicture of life and love,
Oft endurance borne of losses and misery.
These gleams are realization on fond.
Ran on my veins to awful drowsy,
That make me slept to forgetful thoughts.
Bearing nightfall dreams like-
Once upon a time when the world was as young as me.
I'm led to thole, by transit owe.
And to reform the juvenile hypocrisy.
Lo, our omen are physics of many typical form and creation.

55. RETALIATION

A retaliation if her wishes
Is moving swiftly and recurrence.
The lines high upon our head bends
Towards heated blender mill.
Stairs were ever stepped upon
While trying to reach the sparing lance of sight.
With a lace that could bind right and lead,
I see the world as it pretend to be,
But always seeking redressal in a reverse movement.
Under a flat ceiling, door and two windows being locked inward.
I looked at people walking through narrow lane,
In momentariness, hopest against frailer,
Whistle some sort of respite.
Yet, school of wrappers laugh at unknowingly.
In musing notices and surges.
Her wingless wind blow from the smart bay.
Gazing swarm of praying bands,
When I along with trees and leaves prostrate green.
To serve might of lofty Lord.

56. MEMORIES

Long time ago,
We're at school for 8 years long.
And you know, you'd even smile with my hilarious.
Do you remember the day?
When Rahul and I knocked down your cycle down the road,
Supriya and you clumsily say something away from me,
While we're returning from the tinmukh hotel
Back to Sir Ilia's mathematics tution.
Ah, this is a fun to realise childish,
But it oftentimes hurts me as well.
Those little kids who once threatened you calling by my name,
Like Afzal, Shahnawaz and little-little lovely miew,
They are now grown up and I am teaching some of them at school.
Abul, Jaffar, Jaheer were once a naughty kids
But now they understand well learning about life and livelihood
And stop mocking at other rage.
Your sister is quite humiliating,
Her aspiring words were sweets to err but tasted sour.
Rohan and Bikram were lazily supporting me in your case,
But Biramani's favour was soothing to lay off.
And here I remember Thiu demarcation of fours and sixes boundary
apart.
Now, how could I forget the neutral views of omitable Amit and his
brother,

The seriousness of Samsad and Bijon, and dense sense of Dildar.
The smiling face of Giang and silence treat of Tahera.
Rohima was always sad for more than a reason
Arshad the wonder boy, regard his long yesterday' tale to his classmate.
Bulan and Rahuai speaks on loud vocal
Hearing them, Madam Mercy was reasonable to shut their wide mouth.
Big Pradip and Nirola don't disclose their usuality
Yet spoke nurturing and make us laugh like sunny day.
Baby Sana and Rina were quite interesting
However they left us and move further away.
And that boy with an aim, likely to flatter
Is still living in the world hoping for you.

57. TWO HOUSES AND I

Two Houses and I
Lonely is I,
when the late night comes towards me
Its darkness I see,
but lightly as the stars and moon shines above
Under her vastness I lie,
and saw them through every holes of my old roof.
Such poorly living, saidst I
To myself, and seeing my brother and sisters being fulfilled,
I smile and than none of them notice the latent tears.
Sleepily, I felt
Like thinking something about enjoyable daylight
Dawn and dusk friends with little money and loaded pride
But happily when I realised
I'm living in a country
Inside a house with large door and small window
With people either more or less than I.
And fall in sorry
When our countrymen are unlike each other
When their deeds are darker than whiteness
While jealousy over material are brighter than their darkness
Then sadness overwhelmed
Because our community is communal and at other beauty we pretend to
secularize

Because we fear and at other success, we praises their worth.
Because democracy is just words count in our Age-old Constitution
And we are thirst thrice by inflation, lawlessness and toil torment.
So, as the aghast helm.
Seeing the submissive return of
And the victory of
Words are poise and can lie
Therefore connotes the works and proceedings.
Thus, our republic is a defined democracy
Where unity ruled and solemnly ruined
Legislature are elected and not nominated
Unlike the ruly beuracracy, whose dreams make them awake
To be a dignified socialist in our sovereign.

58. THE BLUFFING SUN

The bluffing sun
And it's rays of hope.
Herein found the inspiration of rising against the downfall.
O mighty, Thou shalt hasten your beautification.
Green fishes that jumps moreover the waves,
Yellow birds and red roses that makes a swift morning cries.
But I
Beside your implementation, like a hound
Searches the enlightenment.
Those wealth and luxury, you lead thinking about an able life
When you'd make a heavy rising headway
From your softly provincial matress and banquets balls
Ah! Late than the flutter of His glow worm.
We shall be
At the virgin edge,
We shall remain bare and poor,
To the fate of misfortune and undone.
We shall be guided,
By an electrified frotress leading to a wreck shipyards.
We shall be raid,
By the jealousy of being in proud achievement.
Awake my people!
The lust of sleep on a rainy dawn is more than a payable.
Even by the noon

You sweat and endorse out of your own pride.
Quite in that visible warming
Sufferage of extremities, without prayers will He listen to heeds.
The words of sinners, begging for forgiveness
And the merciless king be seen lying in pitiful auction.
O people; You're betrayed;
Your words were heard, but not Thou wishes,
O listen to my word against many words.
The blood sprouts out to a blush temptation.
But carefully, you'll be a trapped by your angry violence.
So, what will you prefer?
The dominance of falsifying taunts.
Or your true sacrifice that will not be honoured.
Because history is a accords of winners and achievers.

59. IN THE JOY OF APRIL

These are several words.

I thought, I would speak out in the dale,

To my happily dwelling people.

When I saw them eating and drinking in the joy of April.

Beside fruitless flowering trees,

The birds dearly set on singing love song.

Sometimes away and then

I saw there, out in that dale.

Few men in worn, healthily built but weird

Returning from the day labouring with cocktail in hand.

Away from their hardship,

They're speaking about the pick.

The crisis arise without a proper remedy.

The launch of religions against faith.

Resistance of inferior against the superior.

They're growing wilder in near and far.

Their losses are breaved far than their untold suffering,

And brave lives are named after proud sacrifice.

Intellectuals fear the sight of supernatural.

Richness vow to candle and some burn wealthy torch.

While there are people who cries for scientific ledger and argues.

Sciences are searching for mistaken things and avoidable truth to serves.

Poets are highly praised to their poems and songs.

Legislators begged people to remain indoor and excuses towards.

TREMORS

Herbs and timbers remain wet
Down in the rains falling from Lordland.
To serves the immediate call of illness for kindness,
Writing mediate lines in the jealous palm of furious hand.
For love and cooperation shall dwelled together in our happy valley
And people will run towards the house of knowledge.

60. THE 30th FAST

It is the 30ᵗʰ Ramadhan of 1443AH.
Her friend asked her,
"Where is your new dress?
Common see...... These are bought by my pappa,
Aren't they beautiful?"
My legs stopped and there spotted her!
With her few friends playing on the sand.
She just nodded and laugh aloud while replying them,
My brother will bring a trucks of toys, jewelery and new clothes.
From the Vishal and Bigbazaar in Silchar.
When he returned from school taking his salary.
And you know I lay in empty hand.
Two hands that lean to hardwork all 30 long days.
Still than, a dissatisfied payment;
I could see, people of the morning and evening.
They're walking in hurry in orderly satisfaction.
While they care little for a poor fellow, in their services
I hope, I could richly work, but–
my earning a sum of pitiful rower.
The dark sky now sowers
Its little gentle falls.
Above the moving trains that passes through deep woods.
The passenger within welcome her nurture
On carolling trees that moves behind.

A wall beside me promising some greenery,
Children shouts to the turbine of joy
Singing cajole and play by the window shield.
I tried looking back
To the calling of a little girl
Curly hair, silky skin and sweet soft voice resembles.
Laughing heartedly with her playful father.
Timid as the fondness of rabits and witty.
Then the rain stops
White clouds are now moving over the sleeves
Oft loyal men sells on town and cities.
Their come the sells man
With rosy dolls, yellow cars and musical flutes
Putting colours on wants and jeleosy.
But my pocket being poor
I imitate the gentleman who moves round the fair.
But a fatherlike to my sister
Who'd waited hopefully for my returning
With their happy toys they like to play with.
Cosmic lay upon the wonder
For love or for life ahead.
Then a friend of mine.
Who is just there?
Spotted my sorrow and possess me his happy being.
And we used to say, you knows what I know and you don't know that I
don't.
So, no secrecy, lying and cheating between us.

61. THE WIND AND THE POET

Flood!

With its still water,

Laps on the thigh of high raising wounds.

If makes many sorry lives injured to extremities.

From a hill and now from many hills,

In the Barak and its sorrounding,

Through its deepest valley

Over banana trees and banyans.

Flexes honouring the trumpet of lossing,

Under dark skies, lightening and thundering.

Timid soil awakes and raised to walk a little,

Uprootings the living gigantic roots.

So it swallowed, like a thirsty throat and then fill with

Hardship and smells of avenge.

Drops of water from the green mangoes

Is beautiful to look out of shelter's window.

Sitting by the panes and happily wondering about

Easy things and happy living.

When the wind surges into action.

Pathetic felt on rousing of hangs and falls.

Dost of mangoes that once hang in sweetness,

From where raindrops like morning dews impatiently falling,

TREMORS

Is now striving for existance.
Ensuring ability and withstand by enduring fights over powers.
But nature's mights is beyond to measure.
It seems a roaring by the scene of survival
And I see people running down beside the russy river.
Whitness like spikes of clouds on surfaces and plains
Everywhere is the overflowing of water,
Erosion and tragic lashes brown woods and animals sailing impower,
Some hearted men in boat rushes to pull off the chain,
And succeed their mercy mission and they be glorified.
Overnight strength fuses to guess who'd ablaze in anger upon pride.
Civilisation once I belief when he smile at me,
They're thrown in vain and desire into hopelessness,
Losses even swam away from the looser hands.
Fantasy cried littering.
Peebles and rolling sands gathering a swamp.
Often reverine dwellers cheers the multitude,
Their boats rowing in search of highland,
To tent around a safeland.
Unlike winter camp, they're moves to temptation.
Improper dresses they would call for
Help and rescue in their heart
But speak not as their votes are turn to payment instead of choosen.
For several times he would not hear untill the meditator draw the climax.
Than chopper pilots on skies sneering the suffering plights.
Dropping baggage of grains and aids.
Such that victims hands are raised to higher.
A prayer for their victory and indeed acclaim of trustworthy.
This is my land and here refers-

To the wind whistling.
A whistle that everyone sees and says.
Works are twitter in the race to publicize among the worshippers,
And name and address plates lasts longer than work and welfare.

62. Barakki Lepnaidraba Echel

(Feebanda tongjaba khunjaa singdi,
Nongthk-nonghum na phara-phara hairaba auukangda tongba
cheklagum.
Wamankhraduna nokchaba upai audrabsing,
Pukninggi achikpada murum-murum lijahau_e akibagi tengthakhol,
Barakki leiraina knada teinarkhini khlbada.
Adubu taabiraroi knanasu meoibagi athenbana ningthijabda saidongi
Bishwa gi sumhatpolang aronbada.
Tannari meyamna satchage nungaina.
Tau_e_gumbasung ngasigise, mitlugi pirang maronna
Echou kaaraba barakki namthak kallaba echelda luplubgi cheikholni.)
O hear me;
The midnight rain.
The tanks are overflowed and pots are filled,
I'm wet inside my cottage, fear and cold of sickness
Thunder aloud and lightening sparks across the gut.
The guilty heart full of pride and greed,
Who'd utter now and than 'O Lord.'
Fear and panic,
I'd wonder and a reflection of-
my intrinsic, it touches the cornerstone.
O kindness, rain in summer
But this blessing turns more to anger arouse and existing.
This pouring and heavy erosion,

This downpour and high raised floods,

Submerged the land we created inside expensive wall.

And bury living men and cosmic.

Proud and humble alike.

Is this a kind of crush?

Upon those who try to create their empire.

Beside their living in Your kingdom.

With satisfaction, full of freedom.

Imagination is cheap and everyone could afford

So, some man would make Your Image,

And try to create Your pictures.

Would they be believer?

Omnipotent is Thou, so who can affords faith unseen and malignant.

When we are all Your creations.

Even the rains, stroms and floods.

Even the wreck men and their wrecked houses.

Tiring down shall highly praised and prayers

For help and cure over indices against the bitter bites

But it is a happiness,

When the slowing down of dusty water

Down the sandy floors.

Revival of grassy banks in its greening,

Tempered the gloomy glimpses.

Fisherman and sowers will sail handful of harvest,

The blue waters and kindness will provide their daylight.

(Lines inside the brackets are composed in manipuri dilects. It speaks

about the hardship faced by the residents of Barak Valley in the Assam

flood of June, 2022. I, being a victims describes this lyrics is not noted on

feeling or on seeing beauties, but this is an expression of some unbearable torment but forced to bear the same and lived hopefully with the existing. The title "Barakki Lepnaidraba Echel" means flawless flow of Barak)

63. THE MOON AND I

The Moon and I

We had a long conversation.

For her beauty and appraisal,

It tooks me a haunces and somewhere haunted.

In a fairy standing, I visualize her there

For long unnoticed, the foreign of thoughts.

But,

This minutes of unsung mind

Took her towards the delve of heart

And there she dwelled.

Calm and quiet.

But,

When this heart is filled with love

And my mouth is dumb with shy.

What could this facial expression be?

In my vision, far than to see.

Nothing more, than to hide my feeling for her.

And speak some laughters and more.

Though readers enjoy such lines in their pensive,

Ledger writs in the sworn of drowsy eyes.

64. THIS LETTER

This letter
wouldn't be suited in a mailbox.
So, will you read like a poem
Written by a bard.
Days are playable in the lights of colours.
Natural and florescence are relaxing and preferable.
But the azan of this dusk reminds me the risks,
Beside death, delay, tiresome of being undone, unfulfilled wandering and
sacrifices.
However hearsay fools all these lovely little things.
Nights are lonely and barren.
Stars and moons are far away though providing.
The solitude of your winning,
My young mind spell no bound of excitement
And may celebrate the height of togetherness
But canst not, as I alone hope for.

65. O LISTENER

O LISTENER
Trees and green harvest.
Worships the devastating nature.
Praising the Almighty Lords,
So that He protect them hearing their prayers.
But I lead their prayer and praise the beauty.
Her hand and heart profound,
Beside beautiful song she sweetly sang,
I kept listening keeping an ear open wide.
O listener, do you hear me.
This is one among my poor song.
I hope to sing together with you.
I tried to speak,
But nonchalantly, words fluttered.
I tried to look,
But shyly, sight turned.
I tried to approach,
But exhaustedly, walks opposing.
Unexpressed desire and due expectation
Would hook me and hover around.

66. THE SMILING HEART

The land that provide me courage
Has taken away, the soul and body apart.
If I'll lay lament, from today onward.
Hardly smiles by the face,
An appearance that everyone belief.

67. DIARY OF 6TH SEPTEMBER

A good morning

When its sky is filled with clouds.

Wet grasses on muddy roads

Filled by the midnight offset and downpour.

The moment is cool and calm

And refreshing all tiredness of the past hardwork.

A bit of deaf shower is enchanting

That drench me to bitter cold.

When the sun rose

Above the horizon.

That reddish lines in the northern sky,

Fades slowly to bluish about.

But this heart convey in silence.

Relays to violence and feels to move out.

Away from the ribs that hold it tight.

And moves along the rays of whistling wind.

68. SULTANATE

69. WANDERER

This rain, the dark skyline, the cool breeze,
After the sunny daylight.
Moved by soft splash on sandy floor.
I wonder this magnificent be,
In this evening little lit.
Those dried and yellow leaves.
Scattered down slowly and steadily,
With these heavenly pouring;
Falling amain, beside your temptation,
I wander if thee be the sole of glimpse.
The multitude of being solitary.
The rolls of rolling water flew in her swiftness.
Timid steps and footmarks on the muddy floor.
Soft splashes made of droplets on your legs.
Brightness as thine walk upon, I see beauties behind the minutes of
running water.
Shyly smiles and thou slowing as we faces upon.
The rainy roads and soften eve.
Your moving ahead and I walks opposing.
Later turning fro though not submissive.
Leaving this sudden moment as a long touch.

70. MIGHT

The lost of linen;

And this angel's heart,

Wept in bitterness o'er de flow of burdens.

Sympathetically revive the stuff I'd loved.

The fairy I met, in her land.

Fair and praise to me, she'll be the queen,

Crown with loves and cares.

Beside the jewels I earned.

Hard to my living, that owe to me and lone I strive.

O Lord!

Unto Your pleasure, I knell down and worships.

I wish I'm one among Your choosen blesses.

I wonder for, this long and pale way,

That soft and tuning pretty.

Steady music, heard on the heart and it's hastening beats.

Slowly, your approaches annexed my calm

Being tempered, I tried to show, how much

But you did feel, I failed to treat and retreated.

Your fallin and trying to running still

Again and again.

I stood high, to hold you tight

Bow low, and look down the leverage,

Waited for your stretching

Deep within, hope and high rises.

You did see me.
I tried to make you feel, it's me;
O come and say, "let's be together and forever we'll raised."
The might of this endurance remains.
But, I fear
If I'll lost your faith and trust.

71. THE TRAVELOGUE

The journey.
Between compiling memories and defining future,
Is a long way to travelled within a short while.
My prayers and your acceptance.
Those few minutes, we'd spend together.
It is the joy of immense that I'll celebrate for years.
I wish to say something more than expressions.
But I find, nothing is sweetest as your presence.
And thank the Lord for comforting me with beauty and beings.
This dark tunnels and within the train.
Around the smoke topped mountains.
And Feeling of fears of seperation but I see some hope in this journey.
This deep valleys and wildering stream,
Below the blue hills.
Arose my misery, but I find myself nearing towards the approaching
gleams
Those hills and it's people
Chants of its children at our moving.
It's slanting roofs shook down on us.
Residental quater and the white blooms of approaching winter,
There I find, I'm taking away the heart of many dedicated learners
Though I left mine in their field.
Deep creek beIow the halves, returning to their inlet bay,
They take their loves from the hall of undergrowth,

And share with their living beings.
Chimneys and runoff,
From the producing mills,
Lay the coolness aside from the morning glee.
And I'm returning unfulfilled.
To my homeland, the land of love and endurance.
From their land, the land of sufficient pride.
This is life, where history is written by vitorious.
This is life where struggler wails against the finishing line.

72. THE UNION OF TWO CROWNED HEART

Man in happiness
Smiles to his glory.
He walks with pride,
Telling a short piece of lifeline
And paid his hardly earned to family's needs and purposes.
The maintainance with love and care he deserves.
Perhaps a mother is
A woman who was once a beautiful lady,
An obedient wife to a goodman,
Her keen to do with loving son and daughter as desires.
Indeed there dwelled her celebration.
In a family who understand her worth.
Marriage is the union of these crowned heart.
The angels brought a fulfillment,
To two wonderers travelling lone unto a preserved destination.
From faraway to the unity against impediments.
The Lords stretches his benight upon His immortal being
And bless their relationship to eternal.

73. THE APPOLOGY

An appology,
I wrote and for the first time.
Asking for a pardon and forgiveness.
Because I am a lay boy.
Who always risked his life,
And enjoy the adventure of endless effort.
But here, I failed and lost.
It made me fallen in the latent depth of pain.
It made me realise the tragic of natural wreckage.
Words are easy to say.
The more it is lightly spoken,
Heavier I felt in maintaining it.
Standing here and watching you,
There and your happy being,
Without the desire, I walks wiping.
I looks to and fro, left and right.
I could see no one, but gathering around me,
Waiting for my hands to leaps them a step and steps higher.
I'm not alone, the stars and moon too,
Watches you and your sleepy night.
The sun and her flowers too gather here.
Just to listen as you say.
Unfaithful tales, inexpressible beside expression, lorn beneath affection.
Cunning and jealous o'er your taken by someone else.

Is this the love without affair?
This feeling that once brought a facial smile.
And now a tainted of its kind.
That hurt me extreme,
Let me lay intoxicated all along the grey lane.
And I'm force to walk along the guided way.

74. THE BADASS

I'm Papu, the badass.

Who leads a carefree leading, free from parenting.

Sometime I bloom life a flower and oft plucked off to disheartening cries.

And like a bird I'll fly, I thought;

To see the adventorous world and their affairs.

But i fear, if I be knocked, who will be responsible to their needs.

I grew amongst love and care.

Without wants but full of fulfilment,

And merry is my childhood, chosen to be the prior son.

But this is life, living in a transit.

Elderly left for heavenly abode,

And vested their responsiblity upon my labour.

Quietly shall i weep,

And loudly I will laugh,

Just to say 'Alhamdulillah for everything.'

Thank You

<u>THANK YOU</u>

www.ingramcontent.com/pod-product-compliance
Lightning Source LLC
Chambersburg PA
CBHW021227130726

47988CB00002B/861